LOVE Fat Quarter QUILTS

20 Delightful Precut Projects for All Skill Levels

T0243766

stashBOOKS.

an imprint of C&T Publishing

Text, photography, and artwork copyright © 2022
by *Love Patchwork & Quilting* Magazine / Immediate Media

Publisher: Amy Barrett-Daffin

Creative Director: Gailen Runge

Senior Editor: Roxane Cerda

Editor: Jennifer Warren

Cover/Book Designer: April Mostek

Production Coordinator: Zinnia Heinzmann

Photography Assistant: Gabriel Martinez

Front cover photography by *Love Patchwork & Quilting*
Magazine / Immediate Media

Photography by *Love Patchwork & Quilting* Magazine / Immediate Media, unless
otherwise noted

Published by Stash Books, an imprint of C&T Publishing, Inc., P.O. Box 1456,
Lafayette, CA 94549

Library of Congress Control Number: 2022940872

Printed in the USA

10 9 8 7 6 5 4 3 2 1

contents

PIXEL DIAMONDS
Karen Lewis

Make a statement with this bright, bold quilt.

TOP TIP
If you cut your binding fabric strips at 2½in wide, instead of 2½in, you will only need ½yd of fabric instead of ¾yd—leaving more fabric for next time!

PRINT AND PATTERN ...
This gorgeous quilt is a mixture of solid fabrics and Karen's own screen-printed designs. Mix and match tonal prints from your stash to get the look!

QUILT

Finished quilt: 80in square

Fabrics used: Robert Kaufman Kona solids, some of which were screen printed by Karen

You Will Need

Fabric Colour 1 (pinks): Five fat eighths in total, made up of different shades

Fabric Colour 2 (yellows): Five fat quarters in total, made up of different shades

Fabric Colour 3 (blues): Nine fat quarters in total (2½yds) in at least four different shades

Fabric neutral/white: At least 3yds in total, made up of different shades

Batting: 90in square

Backing fabric: At least 84in square (5yds approx)

Binding fabric: ¾yd

NOTES

- For this pattern, a fat eighth is assumed to be 11in × 18in (must be a minimum of 10in).
- Press all fabrics well before cutting.
- Seam allowances are ¼in, unless otherwise noted.
- Press seams open unless otherwise instructed.
- HST = half-square triangle

With such a colourful quilt top, a plain backing fabric is ideal for finishing off this project.

Cutting Out

1. From the following fabrics, cut 5in squares for the half-square triangles. You need 204 squares in total.

- Colour 1 fabrics (pinks)—cut 28.
- Colour 2 fabrics (yellows)—cut 52.
- Colour 3 fabrics (blues)—cut 108.
- Neutral/white fabrics—cut 16.

2. For the whole squares, cut 196 4½in squares from neutral/white fabrics.

3. For the binding, cut eight 2½in strips across the width of the fabric. If you only have ½yd for the binding, cut the strips 2¼in wide.

Triangle Units

4. The 5in squares you have cut are all made into half-square triangle units (HSTs)—a total of 204 units. Pair up the squares as follows.

• 8 full Colour 1 (pinks) HSTs

• 6 dark/pale Colour 1 (pinks) HSTs

• 22 full Colour 2 (yellows) HSTs

• 8 Colours 2/3 (yellows/blues) HSTs

• 44 Colour 3 (blues) HSTs

• 14 neutrals/whites HSTs

5. Sew each pair of squares to create half-square triangle units. On one square of each pair, draw a diagonal line from corner to corner. Pin the two squares right sides together. Sew ¼in away from the marked diagonal line on each side. Cut the triangles apart on the marked line. Press the units and then trim each one to 4½in square.

6. Check all of your HSTs are 4½in square and that you have the following units:

• 28 HSTs in Colour 1 (pinks)

• 44 HSTs in Colour 2 (yellows)

• 16 HSTs in Colour 2/3 (yellows/blues)

• 88 HSTs in Colour 3 (blues)

• 28 HSTs in Colour 3 / neutral (blues/neutrals)

Sewing the Units Together

7. Arrange the 4½in HSTs and 4½in neutral squares as shown. If you keep the four quarters of the quilt separate and then sew them together in sections, you will find it more manageable.

TOP TIP

Assemble all of the units into four identical quarters to make the layout shown in the diagram, or change the layout of each quarter as you wish to form a layout of your choice. If you want to play around with the layout, then you may have to make a few extra units.

8. To create the layout shown in the diagram (page 10), sew each quarter of the quilt separately, sewing ten HSTs in each row. Press the seams open. Now sew the ten rows together and press the seams open. Repeat to make the other three-quarters of the quilt top.

Assembling the Quilt

9. Lay out the four quarters as shown. Sew the top two quarters together and press the seam open. Sew the bottom two quarters together and press the seam open. Now sew the two halves together to complete your quilt top.

Quilt layout: Keep all four quarters the same (as shown), or mix it up and arrange your blocks slightly differently for each.

Quilting and Finishing

10. Cut and piece your backing fabric as needed to create a square about 84in–86in. Make a quilt sandwich of the backing fabric, right side down; the batting; and the quilt top, right side up. Smooth the layers and then pin or spray baste them together.

11. Quilt as desired. The quilt shown was quilted in a cross-hatch pattern and then quilted in close lines around the outside of the design to highlight this area.

12. Trim off the excess batting and backing fabric, and square up the quilt ready for binding. Join the binding strips together into one long length and use this as a double-fold binding for your quilt.

TOP TIP

For a small lap quilt, just make the middle diamond section—once finished, it will measure about 40in square.

Karen's daisy print is used on both blue...

...and this pretty pink colour.

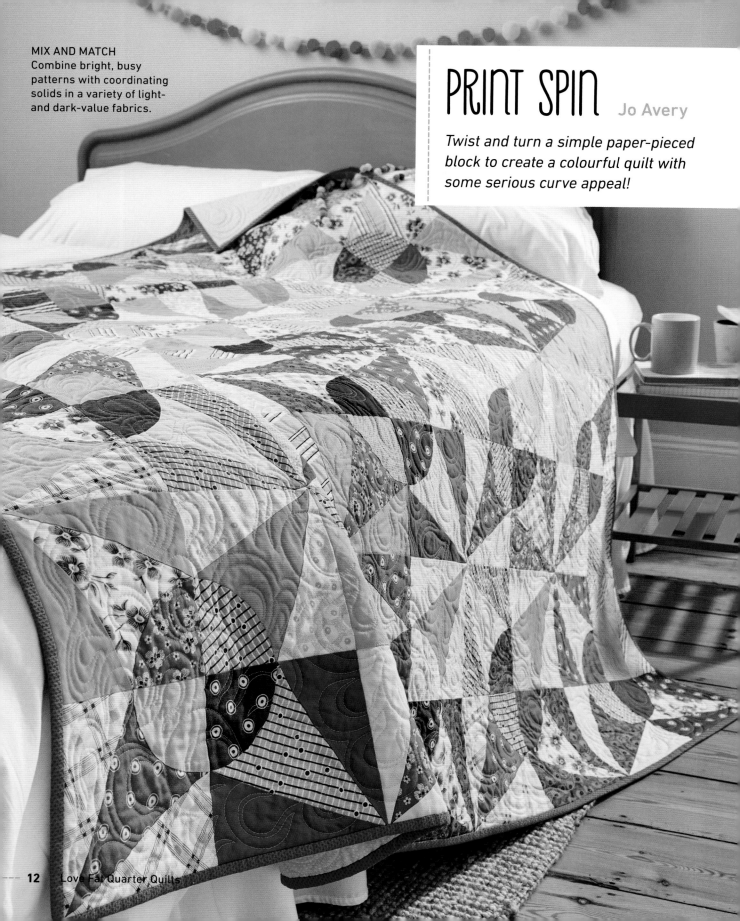

PRINT SPIN Jo Avery

*Twist and turn a simple paper-pieced
block to create a colourful quilt with
some serious curve appeal!*

QUILT

Finished quilt: 70in square

Fabrics used: Fat quarter bundle from Denyse Schmidt's Washington Depot collection by FreeSpirit Fabrics, plus matching solids

You Will Need

A selection of different print and solid fabric with a mixture of light, dark, and medium values: 8yds total (approx thirty two [32] fat quarters)

Batting: 74in square

Backing fabric: 4¼yds

Binding fabric: ⅝yd

FPP Template A: One hundred (100) copies

Template B: One (1) copy

NOTES

- Seam allowances are ¼in throughout, unless otherwise noted.
- Press seams open, unless otherwise instructed.
- Adjust stitch length to 1.5mm for FPP.
- Templates include outer seam allowances only.
- For templates, see Downloadable Patterns (page 93).
- FPP = foundation paper piecing
- WOF = width of fabric
- RST = right sides together
- WST = wrong sides together
- To achieve the effect shown in this quilt, each section of each block is made with dark and light fabrics alternating in the large centre wedge.

Cutting Out

1. From your selection of solid and patterned fabrics, cut:

- One hundred (100) Template B. Save the remaining fabric for FPP Template A.

2. From your binding fabric, cut:

- Eight (8) 2½in × WOF strips

Assembling the Quilt

3. Trim a piece of fabric large enough to cover all of Section 1 on FPP Template A, plus ¼in all the way around. Pin in place on the unprinted side of your template.

4. Cut a contrasting piece of fabric large enough to cover all of Section 2, plus ¼in all the way around. Place RST with the Section 1 fabric and pin along the line between Sections 1 and 2. Fold the fabric along the pinned line to check that, when sewn, the fabric will cover Section 2 plus ¼in around. Adjust as necessary, and pin the fabric RST again.

5. Turn your template so the paper side is facing up. Sew along the line between Sections 1 and 2, using a shortened stitch length. Fold the paper away from the sewn line and trim the seam allowance. Unfold the template and press the fabric open.

TOP TIPS

• When foundation paper piecing, make sure your stitch length is set to 1.5mm to make it easier to remove the paper once you finish your block. Once you come to joining your blocks together, set your machine back to your normal stitch length.

• Always press your block before adding the next piece to make the final block flat and crisp, and always trim the seam allowance after you've added each new piece.

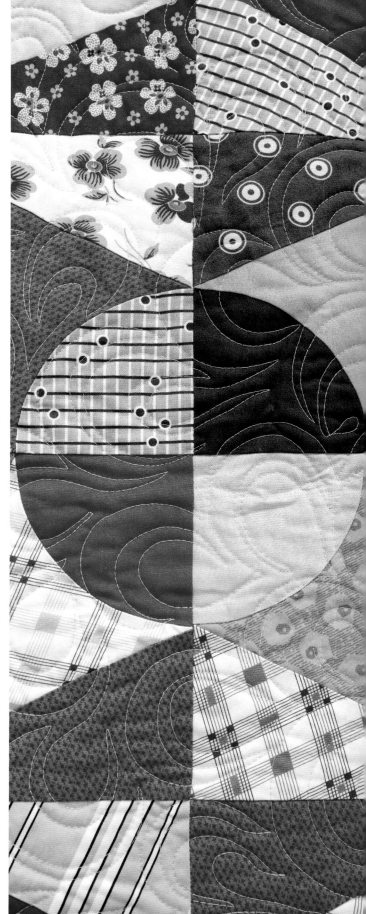

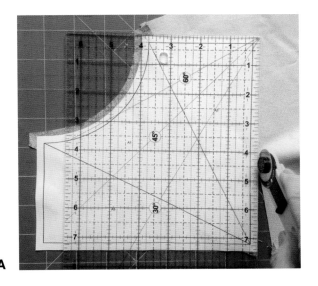

A

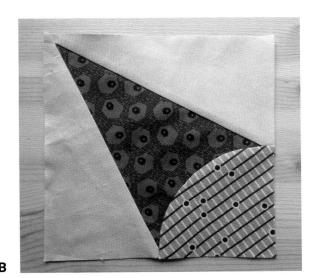

B

6. Repeat Steps 4 and 5 (page 13 and previous page) to cover Section 3 of FPP Template A.

7. Trim along the outer dashed edge of the FPP template. *Fig. A*

8. Take one of the fabric quarter-circles, and with RST, pin to the matching curved edge of the pieced Template A. Sew along the curved edge, carefully and slowly, easing your curved seams and pivoting every few stitches. Press open. *Fig. B*

9. Repeat Steps 3–8 (page 13, previous page, and above) to piece the remaining FPP templates. Add the quarter-circles to complete the quarter-blocks.

10. Remove the paper from the back of each template, tearing along the seamlines. Arrange four quarter-blocks as shown, paying attention to colour placement. Sew the blocks together as you would a Four-Patch block. Repeat to make a total of twenty five (25) blocks. *Figs. C & D*

C

TOP TIP
Separate your blocks into warm and cool colours for a gradual ombré effect.

11. Arrange your blocks in five rows of five. Sew the blocks together in rows. Sew the rows together, carefully matching seams, to complete the quilt top.

D

Finishing the Quilt

12. Cut your backing in half along the width. Sew together along the long edges using a ½in seam. Press open.

13. Press the quilt top and backing well. Make a quilt sandwich by placing the backing fabric right side down, the batting on top, then the quilt top centrally and right side up. The backing and batting are slightly larger than the quilt top. Baste the layers together using your preferred method.

14. Quilt as desired. The quilt shown was free-motion quilted using a mussel variation design.

15. Trim the excess batting and backing level with the quilt top edges, and square up the quilt.

16. Sew the binding strips together end to end using diagonal seams. Press the seams open and trim away the dog-ears. Fold in half lengthwise, WST, and press.

17. Sew the binding to the right side of the quilt, folding a mitre at each corner. Fold the binding over to the back of the quilt and hand stitch in place to finish.

LET'S GET COSY

Susan Standen

Raid your stash for rich, warm prints, and cuddle up with this cosy set this winter.

Four makes for you!

SNUGGLE UP
This lap-size quilt is just the right size for curling up with a good book (and a cup of tea, of course), so treat yourself to a cosy quilt in pretty prints.

QUILT

Finished quilt:
52in × 56in approx

You Will Need

Fabric A (feature print): ½yd

Fabric B (light yellow): Fat quarter

Fabric C (dark yellow): Fat quarter

Fabric D (light pink): Fat quarter

Fabric E (dark pink): Fat quarter

Fabric F (dark red): Fat quarter

Fabric G (orange): Fat quarter

Background fabric (white): 3⅛yds

Backing fabric: 1¾yds (if 56in wide) or 3½yds (if 42in wide)

Batting: 60in × 64in

Binding fabric: ½yd

NOTES

- Seam allowances are ¼in, unless otherwise stated.
- Press seams to the side, unless instructed otherwise.
- FQ = fat quarter
- RST = right sides together
- WOF = width of fabric
- Press all fabrics well before cutting.
- The materials listed for the quilt will produce spare half-square triangle units, which you could use for the mug rug, coffee cosy, and hot water bottle cover.

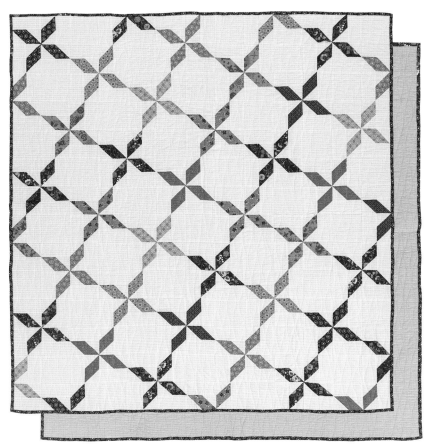

Take care to orient your units as shown to get this pretty windmill effect.

Cutting Out

1. From the background fabric, cut the following:

- Fourteen (14) 4½in × WOF. Subcut into thirty-six (36) 4½in squares and one hundred and forty-six (146) 4½in × 2½in rectangles.

- Nineteen (19) 2½in × WOF strips. Subcut into two hundred and ninety-two (292) 2½in squares.

2. From Fabric A, cut five (5) 2½in × WOF. Subcut into forty (40) 4½in × 2½in rectangles.

3. From Fabrics B, C, D, and E, cut fourteen (14) 4½in × 2½in rectangles from each.

4. From Fabric F, cut twenty (20) 4½in × 2½in rectangles from each.

5. From Fabric G, cut thirty (30) 4½in × 2½in rectangles. You could cut fourteen (14) each from two different oranges if you prefer, as we did.

6. From the binding fabric, cut six (6) 2½in × WOF.

Piecing the Units

> **TOP TIP**
>
> This pattern is ideal for chain piecing. This is when you do the piecing assembly-line style, feeding the next patches for piecing into the feed dogs without breaking the thread from the previous piecing. Continue in this way, then simply snip the threads between each piece afterwards.

7. Take a 2½in × 4½in rectangle and a background (white) 2½in square. Place the white square on the top of the rectangles (right sides together) with three of their edges matching. Sew a line diagonally from the top left corner of the white square to the bottom right corner. *Fig. A*

Now sew another seam approximately ½in away from the first seam. *Fig. B*

8. Cut between the two seams to create two separate units. Press the seam open on both units. The half-square triangle (HST) units aren't used for the quilt but can be saved for the other three smaller projects. *Fig. C*

9. Repeat this with all one hundred and forty-six (146) rectangles and background squares.

10. Repeat this process on all the rectangles with the remaining white squares on the opposite side of the rectangles. Make sure that you sew the seam parallel to the first seam so that when it is pressed open you will have produced a diamond shape, not a Flying Geese shape. *Fig. D*

11. Take the one hundred and forty-six (146) pieced rectangles (half of each colour) and sew a 4½in × 2½in white rectangle to each one, along the long side. It doesn't matter which side you add it to, as the end result will be the same. Once pieced and pressed, you will have one hundred and forty-six (146) 4½in square units. *Fig. E*

Assembling the Quilt Top

12. Set aside ten (10) of the pieced units—these will be needed for the partial units around the edge of the quilt.

- Fabric A (feature fabric), Fabric D (light pink), Fabric E (dark pink), Fabric F (dark red), and Fabric G (orange): two (2) units each

13. Take the remaining units and pair them together with their matching fabrics. Sew each pair together so that two diamond points meet at one end of the seam. *Fig. F*

14. Referring to the quilt photo (page 19), lay out all of the sewn units, the ten (10) units you put aside earlier, and the 4½in squares in rows, taking care to orient the units correctly in fourteen (14) columns.

15. Once you have finalised your layout, then sew each column. Sew the columns together to complete the quilt top.

Quilting and Finishing

16. Prepare a piece of backing fabric about 56in × 60in. Make a quilt sandwich by placing the backing right side down, add the batting, and then the quilt top, right side up. Secure the sandwich layers using your preferred method.

Quilt as desired—the quilt shown was quilted with overlapping wavy lines of stitching.

17. Square up the quilt, trimming excess batting and backing as you do so.

18. Sew the binding strips together end to end and press along the length with wrong sides together. Use this double-fold binding to finish your quilt.

> **TOP TIP: A Trick for Diagonals**
>
> When sewing diagonally across the white squares, it is useful to place a piece of washi tape or masking tape on your machine surface marking a straight line to your needle. If you place the starting corner at the needle and the end corner on the tape line and follow this line with the point as you sew, you will get a nice straight line each time without having to mark a line on each square.

A

B

C

D

This quilt has a simple white background, but grey would look oh-so inviting!

E

F

MUG RUG

Finished mug rug:
7in × 8in

NOTES

• Use the spare HST units from the quilt (page 19) or follow the You Will Need list above and instructions at right.

Perfect for weeny scraps you still treasure.

Making the HST Units

1. Select eight pairs of HSTs left over from the quilt for a total of sixteen (16) HSTs. Alternatively, make HST units as follows.

2. Place a 2in print square right sides together with a 2in white square. Mark a line along the diagonal. Sew a ¼in seam either side of the diagonal line. Cut the squares apart on the diagonal line and press each HST open. Trim the unit down to 1½in square, ensuring that you have the diagonal centred. Repeat to make the rest of the HST units—you need eight pairs in total.

Assembling the Mug Rug

3. Layout the HSTs in columns of diamonds. Place a 1½in square of matching fabric on either side of each diamond and the 2in × 8½in strips of feature fabric on the sides (see photo above for reference). Piece these columns together. Press the seams open.

Quilting and Finishing

4. Make a quilt sandwich from the 8½in square of feature fabric, the batting square, and the patchwork panel, and then quilt as desired. The mug rug was quilted with overlapping wavy lines.

Square up the mug rug and trim the excess backing and batting, and then bind your mug rug to finish.

We think a mug rug with some fancy hot choc and marshmallows makes a lovely gift!

HOT WATER BOTTLE COVER

Finished cover:
12in × 9in

NOTES
• Use the spare HST units from the quilt (page 19) or follow the You Will Need list above and instructions at right.

Get a pro finish with a strip of binding.

Susan's used the most amazing fine pink corduroy—it's such a tactile fabric.

Cutting Out

1. From print fabric, cut the following:

• Two (2) 1½in × 9½in for front of cover
• One (1) 4½in × 9½in for back of cover

2. From background fabric, cut the following:

• Two (2) 6½in × 9½in
• Two (2) 4½in × 9½in
• One (1) 1¼in × 9½in for back of cover

Making the HST Units

3. Select eighteen (18) pairs of HSTs left over from the quilt. Alternatively, make HST units as described in Mug Rug, Step 2 (page 22).

Assembling the Front Panel

4. Lay the eighteen (18) HSTs out to form white diamonds. Sew them together in two rows and then sew the rows together. Press the seams open to reduce bulk.

5. Attach the 1½in × 9½in print fabric strips to the top and bottom of the pieced diamonds strip.

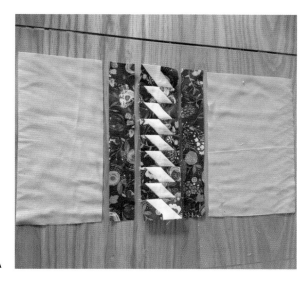

A

B

6. Stitch one of the 4½in × 9½in pieces of background fabric to the bottom of the patchwork, and one of the 6½in × 9½in pieces of background fabric to the top. This will form the front of the cover. *Fig. A*

Assembling the Back Panel

7. Stitch the remaining 4½in × 9½in piece of background fabric to the bottom of the 4½in × 9½in rectangle of print fabric. Stitch the 1¼in × 9½in strip of fabric to the top of the print fabric. This will form the lower back panel of the hot water bottle cover.

Cut a piece of fusible batting the same size and fuse to the back of this lower panel.

8. Cut a piece of fusible batting the same size as the front cover piece and fuse together. Fuse the final piece of batting to the remaining 6½in × 9½in piece of fabric (which will form the upper back panel of the cover).

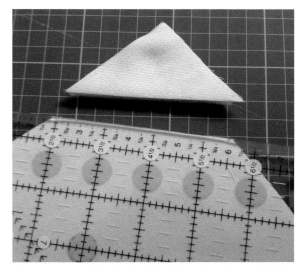

C

9. Attach the binding along the 9½in edge of the upper back panel. *Fig. B*

10. Use an overlock stitch or a zigzag stitch to finish the top edge of the bottom back panel (along the narrower strip of backing fabric).

11. Take the upper back panel and mark 2½in in from each top corner. Using these marks as guides, trim a triangle from one corner. *Fig. C*

Repeat on the other corner. *Fig. D*

12. Repeat this process with the front panel to cut triangles from the top corners.

D

Assembling the Cover

13. Using a small glass or other circular object, trim all the corners of the front panel.

Repeat for the four trimmed corners on the upper back panel and the bottom two corners of the lower back panel. *Fig. E*

14. Sew one side of the hook-and-loop tape to the wrong side of the top section of the lower back panel, positioning it in the centre of the panel. Sew the corresponding piece of hook-and-loop tape to the bottom edge of the upper back panel, just in from the binding.

15. Lay the front of the cover on a flat surface, right side up. Place the upper back piece on top, right side down and matching the top edges. Put the lower back piece on top, right side down and matching the lower edges of the front of the cover—it will overlap the other back piece. Pin in place. *Fig. F*

16. Sew all around the edges and then finish with an overlock stitch or a zigzag stitch. Turn the cover the right way out to finish.

E

F

COFFEE COSY

Finished cosy:
10½in × 3½in approx

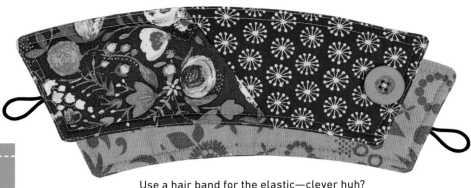

Use a hair band for the elastic—clever huh?

You Will Need

Print fabrics for cosy front:
Two (2) fabrics, each 5in × 8in

Print fabric for cosy back:
5in × 11½in

Batting: 5in × 11½in

Elastic: 3in long

Button: One, about
1in diameter

NOTES
• Seam allowances are ¼in,
unless otherwise stated.

Cutting Out

1. Take Templates A, B, and C (see Downloadable Patterns, page 93) and cut one of each of them from the corresponding pieces of fabric. Cut one Template A from batting. *Fig. A*

Assembling the Coffee Cosy

2. Sew the two smaller pieces (Templates B and C) together along the centre seam. When pinning them together, make sure you offset the corners so that the fabric edges meet ¼in from where your seamline will be. It is useful to pin well on this seam, as it is on the bias. *Fig. B*

3. Place the pieced front of the cosy on the batting and sew ⅛in from the edge all round to fix the pieces together.

A

B

C

D

4. Place the folded elastic on the cosy front with the loop over the fabric on one short end. You can also use a hair elastic with about half of it on the fabric, with the two sides of the elastic touching. Stitch it down with a ⅛in seam—a shorter stitch length and backstitching help ensure the elastic is adequately attached. *Fig. C*

5. Place the backing fabric and pieced front RST. Using a ¼in seam, stitch around the edge, leaving about a 3in gap for turning. Clip the corners. *Fig. D*

6. Turn the cosy the right way out and press, taking care to tuck the raw fabric edges of the turning gap in to match the rest of the cosy. Stitch around the edge to ensure the gap is closed. *Fig. E*

Sew a second row of stitching ¼in in from the edge. *Fig. F*

7. Stitch the button in place on the opposite end of the cosy from the elastic loop.

E

Give your morning coffee an instant style update with a sweet print cosy

F

EARN YOUR STRIPES
Laura Pritchard

This purple colour palette is the perfect winter-warmer.

WINTER WANDERING
What could be better than a long stroll on a chilly winter morning? How about coming home to a cosy quilt and a hot cocoa!

QUILT

Finished quilt:
43¾in × 56¼in approx

NOTES

- Seam allowances are a ¼in, unless otherwise noted.
- RST = right sides together
- WOF = width of fabric
- Read through all steps before cutting or sewing.
- Refer to the cutting plans (pages 33 and 34) for the most efficient use of fabric.
- Press fabrics well before starting.
- For templates, see Downloadable Patterns (page 93).

Cutting Out

Note: When cutting the Template 1, 2, 3, and 5 stripes, cut your fabric into strips 1⅜in wide, and then use the templates to cut the appropriate lengths.

1. From Fabric A, cut:

- Twelve (12) Template 1
- Two (2) Template 2
- Fourteen (14) Template 3
- Eight (8) Template 5 triangles
- One (1) 2⅜in square, subcut into two Template 5 triangles
- One (1) 7¼in square HST

2. From Fabric B, cut:

- Six (6) Template 1
- Fourteen (14) Template 2
- Five (5) Template 3
- Thirteen (13) Template 4
- Four (4) 2⅜in squares, subcut into eight Template 5 triangles. Cut one more triangle.
- Six (6) 7¼in squares, subcut into twelve HSTs

3. From Fabric C, cut:

- Sixteen (16) Template 1
- Eleven (11) Template 3
- One (1) Template 4
- Four (4) 2⅜in Template 5 triangles
- Three (3) 2⅜in squares, subcut into six Template 5 triangles

4. From Fabric D, cut:

- One (1) Template 1
- Six (6) Template 2
- Four (4) Template 3
- Three (3) Template 4
- Four (4) 2⅜in squares, subcut into eight Template 5 triangles
- Two (2) 7¼in squares, subcut into four HSTs
- Six (6) 2½in × WOF strips for binding

5. From Fabric E, cut:

- Five (5) 2⅜in squares, subcut into ten Template 5 triangles
- Twelve (12) Template 1
- Fourteen (14) Template 3

6. From Fabric, F cut:

- Fifteen (15) Template 1
- Fifteen (15) Template 3
- Five (5) 2⅜in squares, subcut into ten Template 5 triangles
- One (1) 2⅜in Template 5 triangle

7. From background fabric, cut:

- One (1) Template 1
- Forty-one (41) Template 2
- Forty-six (46) Template 4
- One (1) 2⅜in Template 5 triangle
- Two (2) 2⅜in squares, subcut into four Template 5 triangles
- Twenty-three (23) 7¼in squares, subcut into forty-six HSTs

Use the key and cutting plans to make the most of your fabric:

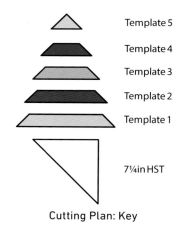

Cutting Plan: Key

> **TOP TIP**
>
> Your background fabric should be the darkest, followed by Fabric A. Fabrics B–F should gradually get lighter/brighter, with F as your lightest fabric.

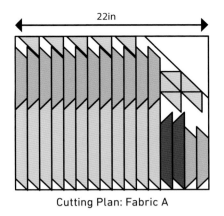

Cutting Plan: Fabric A

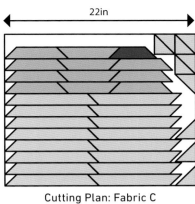

Cutting Plan: Fabric C

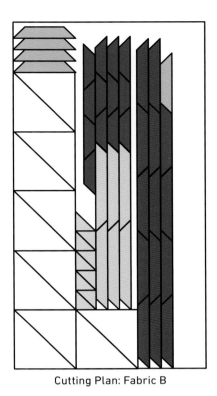

Cutting Plan: Fabric B

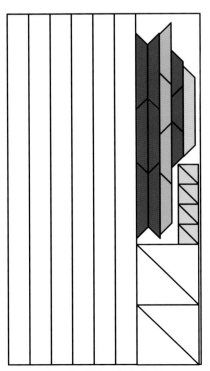

Cutting Plan: Fabric D

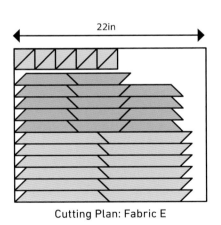

Cutting Plan: Fabric E

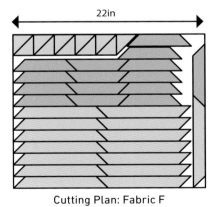

Cutting Plan: Fabric F

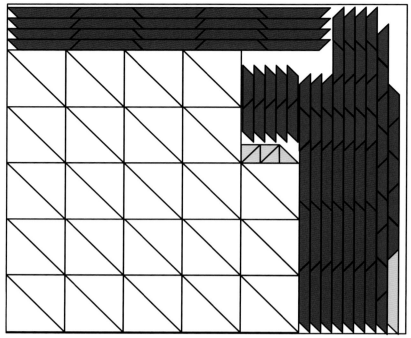

Cutting Plan: Background Fabric

TOP TIP

Lay out all your pieces before sewing to get the most pleasing fabric place-ment. Your blocks should be mostly dark in the centre column, using only one of your darker prints with the solid fabric, graduating out into lighter, more contrasted blocks, and then dispersing out into a mixture of prints to give a more scattered effect around the edges.

Piecing the Quilt Top

8. Each block will need one 7¼in triangle and one of each sized strips 1–5. Assemble your blocks by sewing the strips together in size order to create a striped triangle, as shown. *Fig. A*

9. Sew together your background triangle to the striped triangle to make your square block. Trim the block to 6¾in square. Repeat with the remaining fabric until all sixty-three blocks are made. *Fig. B*

10. Sew your blocks together in nine (9) rows of seven (7) blocks. Join the blocks in rows, pressing seams to one side, alternating direction with each row.

11. Nestle the seams of your rows for matching points, pin, and sew the rows together. Press seams open or to one side.

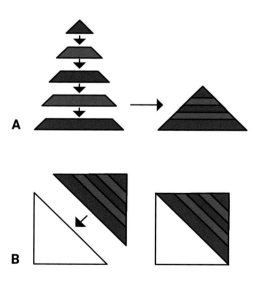

Quilting and Finishing

12. Make a quilt sandwich and baste using your preferred method. Quilt as desired. The quilt shown was quilted with a meandering line throughout all the large background triangles.

13. Sewing your binding strips together end to end. Press the seams open and then fold the whole strip in half WST lengthways. Use to bind your quilt.

> ### TOP TIP
> A palette of rich jewel tones is perfect for making skinny stripes of fresh summer shades, like mint green and aqua, really pop in your blocks!

Green and aqua stripes pop on purple fabric.

PIXEL POP

Felice Regina

Take inspiration from bright and beautiful tiles with a geometric design that fizzes with fresh, zingy colours.

COOL & CRISP
Blocks of bright colour sing when set in a simple pattern against a clean white background.

QUILT

Finished quilt: 66in square

TOP TIP

Quilt a free-motion pattern of abstract rectangles to match the angular design.

You Will Need

Background fabric: 4¼yds

Navy fabric:
One (1) 10in square

Pink fabric:
Three (3) fat quarters

Yellow fabric:
Two (2) fat quarters

Aqua fabric:
Two (2) fat quarters

Backing fabric: 4⅛yds

Batting: 74in square

Binding fabric: ½yd

NOTES

- Seam allowances are ¼in, unless otherwise noted.
- Press seams to one side, unless otherwise instructed.
- WOF = width of fabric
- LOF = length of fabric
- WST = wrong sides together
- Long strips are cut lengthwise along the fabric. If you wish to cut WOF strips and piece them together, you may need less fabric than listed.

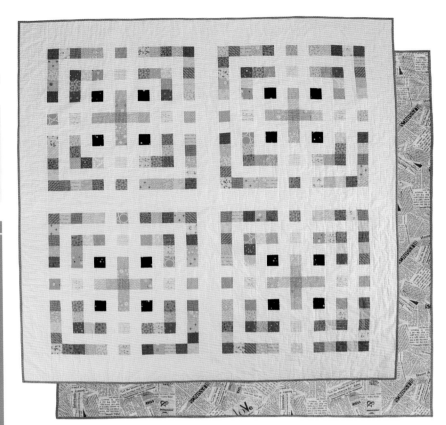

Cutting Out

1. From the background fabric, cut:

- One (1) 14½in × WOF strip. Subcut into eight (8) 2½in × 14½in strips and eight (8) 2½in × 10½in strips.

- Eight (8) 2½in × WOF strips. Subcut into eight (8) 2½in × 10½in strips, eight (8) 2½in × 14½in strips, and eight (8) 2½in × 4½in pieces.

- Two (2) 4½in × length of fabric (LOF) strips (approx 110in). Subcut into one (1) 4½in × 56½in strip and two (2) 4½in × 26½in strips.

- Four (4) 5½in × LOF strips (approx 110in). Subcut into two (2) 5½in × 66½in strips, two (2) 5½in × 56½in strips, and eighty (80) 2½in squares.

- Four (4) 2½in × LOF strips (approx 110in). Subcut into eight (8) 2½in × 22½in strips, eight (8) 2½in × 18½in strips, and eight (8) 2½in × 4½in pieces.

2. From the navy fabric, cut:

- Sixteen (16) 2½in squares

3. Organise your pink fabrics into dark, medium, and light, and cut:

- Forty eight (48) dark 2½in squares

- Thirty two (32) medium 2½in squares

- Thirty two (32) light 2½in squares

4. Organise your yellow fabrics into dark and light, and cut:

- Thirty two (32) dark 2½in squares

- Fifty two (52) light 2½in squares

5. Organise your aqua fabrics into dark and light, and cut:

- Forty eight (48) dark 2½in squares

- Forty eight (48) light 2½in squares

6. From the binding fabric, cut:

- Seven (7) 2½in × WOF strips

Piecing the Quadrants

7. Arrange nine yellow squares, four navy squares, four background squares, and four 2½in × 4½in background pieces, as shown. *Fig. A*

Sew the squares together, pressing the seams away from the centre in rows one, three and five, and towards the centre square in rows two and four.

8. Sew the rows together, nesting the seams. Press the seams open.

9. Sew 2½in × 10½in background strips to the top and bottom of the block you just made. Press the seams away from the quilt centre. Next, sew a 2½in × 14½in background strip to either side, and press the seams away from the centre.

10. Use twenty aqua squares, four yellow squares, and eight background squares to make four border strips, arranging as shown. *Fig. B*

Sew the top and bottom borders, pressing the seams towards the yellow centres. Sew the side borders, pressing the seams away from the centre.

11. Sew the top and bottom borders to the block, pressing the seams towards the quilt centre. Sew the remaining borders to the sides of the block, pressing the seams towards the quilt centre.

12. Sew 2½in × 18½in background strips to the top and bottom of the block. Press the seams away from the centre. Sew a 2½in × 22½in background strip to either side, pressing the seams away from the centre.

13. Make the final borders, using twenty eight pink squares, four aqua squares, eight yellow squares, and eight background squares. *Fig. C*

Sew the top and bottom borders together, pressing the seams towards the central aqua squares. Sew the side borders, pressing the seams away from the centre.

14. Sew the top and bottom borders to the block, pressing the seams towards the quilt centre. Sew the remaining borders to the sides of the block, pressing the seams towards the quilt centre.

15. Repeat Steps 7–14 (above) to make a total of four quadrant pieces.

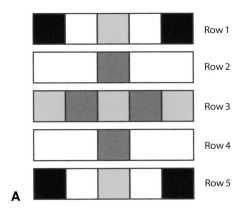

A

Row 1
Row 2
Row 3
Row 4
Row 5

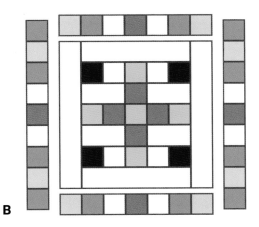

B

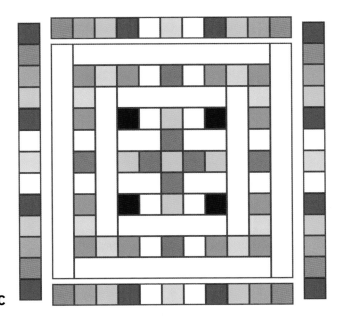

C

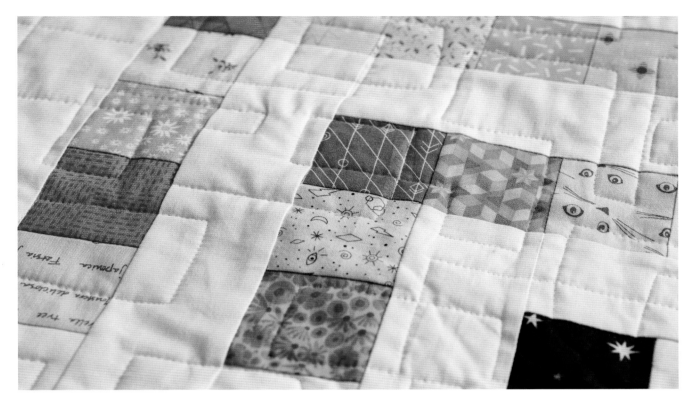

Assembling the Quilt Top

16. Arrange your quadrants into pairs, and sew a 4½in × 26½in background strip vertically between pairs, referring to the layout diagram (at right). Press the seams towards the background strip.

17. Sew the two pairs together, inserting a 4½in × 56½in background strip between the two units. Press the seams towards the background strip.

18. Sew 5½in × 56½in background strips to the top and bottom of the quilt top, pressing the seams away from the centre. Sew the 5½in × 66½in background strips to the sides of the quilt top, pressing the seams away from the centre of the quilt.

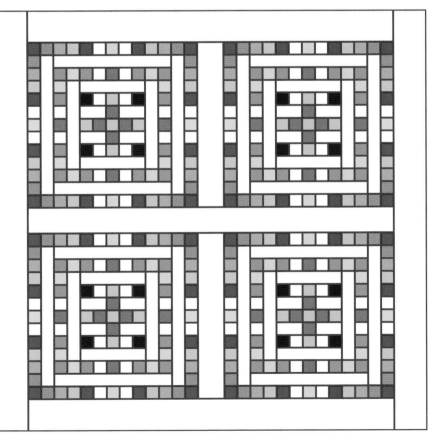

Quilt layout

Quilting and Finishing

19. Cut the backing fabric in half across the width. Remove the selvedges and sew the two pieces together using a ½in seam. Press the seam open.

20. Press the quilt top and backing well. Make a quilt sandwich by placing the backing fabric right side down, the batting on top, then place the quilt top centrally and right side up. Baste the layers together using your preferred method.

21. Quilt as desired. The quilt shown was quilted in abstract rectangles in white thread to mirror the angular patchwork design. Trim off the excess batting and backing fabric, and square up the quilt.

22. Sew the binding strips together end to end using diagonal seams. Press the seams open and trim any dog-ears. Fold in half lengthways, wrong sides together, and press.

23. Sew the binding to the right side of the quilt, creating a neat mitre at each corner. Fold the binding over to the back of the quilt and hand stitch in place around the edge to finish.

MINI QUILT

Finished quilt: 15in square

Transform one quadrant block into a colourful cushion or mini quilt.

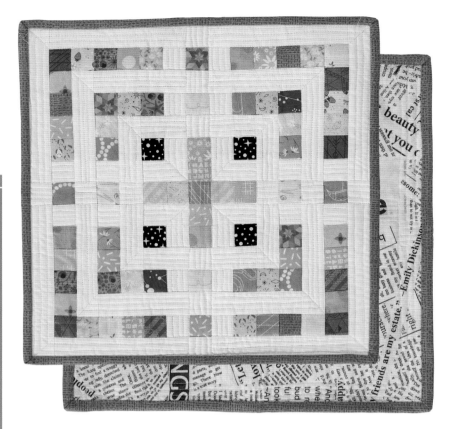

You Will Need

Background fabric: ¼yd

Navy fabric: One (1) 5in square

Pink fabric: Three (3) 10in squares

Yellow fabric: Two (2) 10in squares

Aqua fabric: Two (2) 10in squares

Backing fabric: One (1) fat quarter

Batting: 18in square

Binding fabric: ¼yd

Cutting Out

1. From the background fabric, cut:

- Five (5) 1½in × WOF strips. Subcut into twenty (20) 1½in squares, four (4) 1½in × 2½in strips, two (2) 1½in × 5½in strips, two (2) 1½in × 7½in strips, two (2) 1½in × 9½in strips, two (2) 1½in × 11½in strips, two (2) 1½in × 13½in strips, and two (2) 1½in × 15½in strips.

2. From the navy fabric, cut:

- Four (4) 1½in squares

3. Organise your pink fabrics into dark, medium, and light, and cut:

- Twelve (12) dark 1½in squares
- Eight (8) medium 1½in squares
- Eight (8) light 1½in squares

4. Organise your yellow fabrics into dark and light, and cut:

- Eight (8) dark 1½in squares
- Thirteen (13) light 1½in squares

5. Organise your aqua fabrics into dark and light, and cut:

- Twelve (12) dark 1½in squares
- Twelve (12) light 1½in squares

6. From the binding fabric, cut:

- Two (2) 2½in × WOF strips

Piecing the Mini Quilt Top

7. See Piecing the Quadrants, Steps 7–14 (page 39) to piece the mini quilt top. Sew a 1½in × 13½in background strip to the top and bottom of the quilt top, pressing the seams away from the centre. Sew a 1½in × 15½in background strip to either side, pressing the seams away from the centre again.

Quilting and Finishing

8. Make a quilt sandwich by placing the backing fabric right side down, the batting on top, then place the quilt top centrally and right side up. Baste the layers together using your preferred method.

9. Quilt as desired. The quilt shown was quilted in straight lines roughly ¼in apart. Trim any excess and square up the mini quilt.

10. Sew the binding strips together end to end using diagonal seams. Press the seams open. Fold in half lengthways, WST, and press. Sew the binding to the right side of the quilt, creating a mitre at each corner. Fold over to the back and stitch in place.

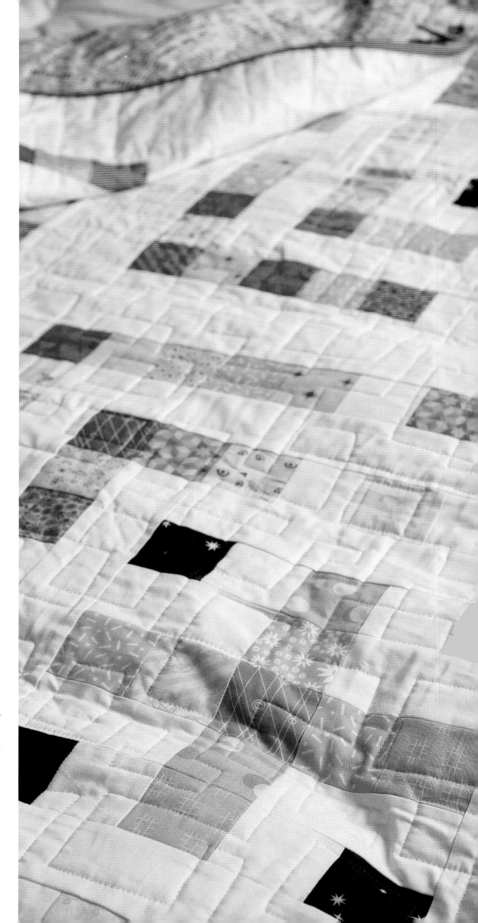

HOURGLASS TWIST

Karen Lewis

This simple quarter-square triangle design lets your fabric do the talking!

GREY ABBEY
Elizabeth Olwen's debut collection for Cloud 9 fabrics is delightful. Each of the prints is beautiful in it's own right, but when you put the whole collection together... well, it's a little bit magic!

QUILT

Finished quilt:
44in × 64in approx

Fabric used: All of the print fabrics shown are from the Grey Abbey collection by Elizabeth Olwen for Cloud 9.

You Will Need

Fat quarters for the 4½in squares: Six (6) of different designs

Fat quarters for the hourglass blocks: Ten (10) of different designs

Batting: 50in × 70in

Backing fabric: 50in × 70in

Binding fabric: ½yd

NOTES

• Seam allowances are ¼in, unless otherwise noted.

• HST = half-square triangle

• Press all fabrics well before cutting.

• Press seams open, unless otherwise instructed.

The striking Swaying Floral print in Egg Blue is darker than the rest of the range—ideal for binding.

Cutting Out

1. Cut eighty-eight (88) 4½in squares from the six (6) fat quarters (about fifteen squares from each fat quarter).

2. Cut eighty-eight (88) 6in squares from the ten (10) fat quarters (about nine squares from each fat quarter).

3. Cut seven (7) 2½in strips from the binding fabric.

Use a single collection for easy colour-matching.

Making the Hourglass Blocks

4. Pair the 6in squares with right sides facing, and use a ruler and a fabric pen to mark a diagonal line across each of the fabric pairs. Sew the squares together ¼in either side of the marked line. Repeat for all pairs.

5. Cut the triangles apart on the marked line. *Fig. A*

Press the units open, with the seam to one side, and repeat for all pairs. You should now have eighty-eight (88) HSTs.

6. Pair two HSTs together, aligning the seams. Draw a diagonal line across each pair, perpendicular to the HST. *Fig. B*

If you prefer a more uniform design, pair two identical HSTs with contrasting triangles facing each other. Or for four random fabrics, pair two unmatching HSTs from your pile.

7. Sew ¼in along either side of your marked line, as you did before. Repeat for all your blocks.

Cut across the marked line and press your units open and trim to 4½in square. *Fig. C*

You should now have eighty-eight (88) hourglass blocks. *Fig. D*

> ### TOP TIP
> Making hourglass blocks is simple. Just line up the seams of two half-square triangles, sew, and cut on the opposite diagonal for two perfect blocks.

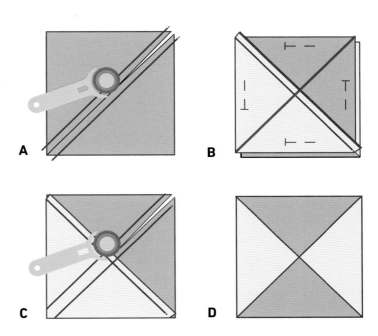

A B

C D

Assembling the Quilt Top

8. Arrange the Hourglass blocks and plain 4½in squares in sixteen rows of eleven, alternating a plain square with an Hourglass block, referring to the layout diagram.

9. Sew the blocks together in rows. Press the seams open and then sew the rows together, again pressing the seams when you are done.

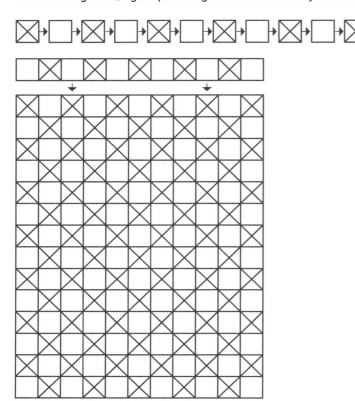

Quilt layout: Alternate your Hourglass blocks and fabric squares along each row, as shown.

Quilting and Finishing

10. Make a quilt sandwich of the backing fabric, right side down; the batting; and the quilt top, right side up. Smooth the layers and then pin or spray baste them together. Quilt as desired.

The quilt shown was quilted diagonally through all the squares, highlighting the hourglass shape.

11. Trim off the excess batting and backing fabric, and square up the quilt ready for binding. Join the binding strips together into one long length and press right sides together. Use this as a double-fold binding for your quilt.

CUSHION

Finished cushion:
19in square

You Will Need

Solid fabric:
One (1) fat quarter

Patterned fabrics:
Four (4) different fabrics
12in square each

Batting: 25in square

Muslin (US) or calico (UK):
25in square

Backing fabric: 20in × 25in

Binding fabric: 2½in × 20in

Wide ribbon: 3in (*optional*)

Cushion pad: 20in square

Use a solid fabric for the plain fabric squares to really bring out the pattern in the print blocks!

Cutting Out

1. Cut twelve (12) 4½in squares from the solid fat quarter.

2. Cut fourteen (14) 6in squares from the patterned fabrics.

3. Cut your backing fabric into one (1) 20in × 14in piece and one (1) 20in × 11in piece.

Making the Hourglass Blocks

4. Make your hourglass blocks as per Quilt, Making the Hourglass Blocks, Steps 4–7 (page 47), using your 6in patterned squares.

5. Arrange your blocks into five (5) rows of five (5), adding in the solid blocks and referring to the layout diagram (at right).

6. Sew your blocks together in rows, pressing the seams in alternate directions for each row. Then sew the rows together.

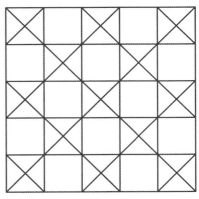

Cushion layout

Quilting and Finishing

7. Layer your muslin, batting, and pieced block to form a quilt sandwich and baste. Quilt as desired and trim to 20in square.

8. Press your binding strip in half, right sides together. Use to bind one edge of your 20in × 14in backing fabric.

9. Press under ½in twice on one long edge of your 20in × 11in backing fabric. Topstitch along the edge to create a double-fold hem.

10. Lay out your quilted cushion top, right side up. Take your ribbon and fold in half, right sides together. Place it on one edge of the cushion, matching raw edges, with the loop facing the center of the cushion. Baste or pin in place.

11. Lay your bound backing piece facedown on your cushion top, aligning the raw edges on the top and sides. Lay your hemmed backing fabric on top, right side down, aligning raw edges with the bottom and sides of the cushion. The two hems should be overlapping in the centre. Pin in place.

12. Sew around the outer edge of the cushion using a ½in seam allowance. Clip the corners and turn right side out. Pop in your cushion pad, and you're done!

TOP TIP

Due to the smaller scale of this coordinating cushion, the fabric choices are minimal, and a solid fabric was added to keep it simple. If you prefer the more random arrangement of the quilt, you could use more prints to achieve the same effect!

CLIPPINGS
Nicole Calver

This super simple mini really lets your fabrics shine!

CORAL'S THE COLOUR
Nothing makes our hearts sing like a pop of coral on a crisp white background!

SUPER-SIZE BLOCK

Finished block:
24in square approx

You Will Need

Fabric A: One (1) fat quarter

Fabric B: One (1) fat quarter

Fabric C: One (1) fat quarter

Background fabric: ½yd

Backing fabric: 29in square

Batting: 29in square

Binding fabric: ¼yd

NOTES

• Seam allowances are ¼in, unless otherwise noted.

• RST = right sides together

• WOF = width of fabric

• HST = half-square triangle

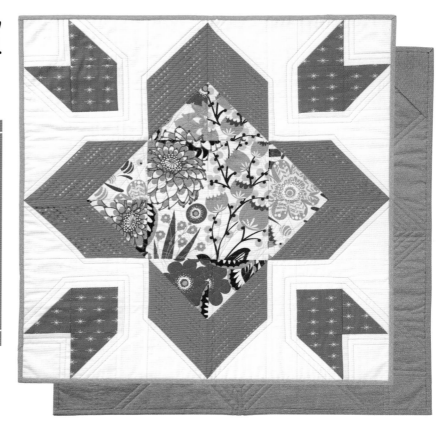

Dense quilting gives your mini structure.

Cutting Out

1. From Fabric A (floral), cut one (1) 8½in square and eight (8) 4½in squares.

2. From Fabric B (yellow), cut four (4) 4in squares and four (4) 3½in squares.

3. From Fabric C (orange), cut eight (8) 8½in × 4½in rectangles.

4. From the background fabric, cut:

• Eight (8) 4½in squares

• Four (4) 4in squares

• Four (4) 3½in squares

• Four (4) 2½in × 8½in rectangles

• Four (4) 2½in × 6½in rectangles

5. From the binding fabric, cut three (3) 2¼in × WOF strips.

A

Block A

6. With your 4in squares of Fabric B and background fabric, sew together using the two-in-one HST method.

With squares RST, draw a diagonal line on the reverse of one square. Sew the squares together ¼in from the drawn line, on both sides. Cut along the line. Press the seams away from the background and square up each HST to 3½in. Repeat to make eight (8) HSTs in total. *Fig. A*

7. Sew two HST units, one 3½in background square, and one 3½in Fabric B square into a four-patch unit. Press seams away from HSTs. Repeat with the remaining HSTs and 3½in squares to make four (4) units. *Fig. B*

8. Now take your 2½in × 6½in rectangles of background fabric and sew to the bottom of your four-patch units, taking care to orient your four-patch units correctly. Press the seams towards the background fabric. *Fig. C*

9. Finally sew your 2½in × 8½in rectangles along the side of your block, again making sure to orient your block correctly before sewing in place. Press the seams towards the background fabric to complete Block A. *Fig. D*

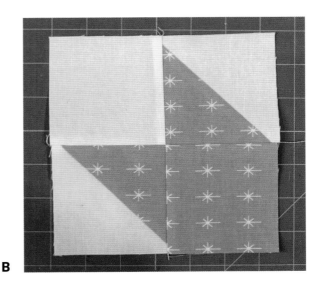

B

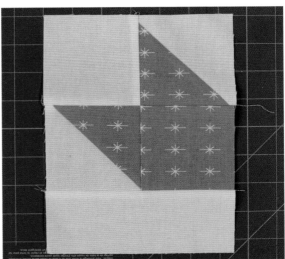

C

D

Block B

10. With RST, place two of the 4½in background squares on the top half of the Fabric C rectangles. Draw a diagonal line from the inside top corner to the outside bottom corner of both background squares. Draw an additional line a ½in on the outside of the line you just made—this will yield HSTs that can be used for another project or the mini quilt. *Fig. E*

Sew along the two lines you've drawn and cut in the middle of them. Open and press away from background. *Fig. F*

11. Repeat with remaining Fabric C rectangles and 4½in background squares. You will have four pairs that mirror each other.

12. Take the eight 4½in squares of Fabric A and place RST on the bottom of your Fabric C rectangles. Draw the same set of lines, making sure they run parallel to the top seam. *Fig. G*

Again, sew along the two lines and cut in the middle. Open and press seams toward Fabric A. *Fig. H*

13. Now sew all four pairs together to make four (4) of Block B. *Fig. I*

Piecing the Quilt Top

14. Using the 8½in square of Fabric A and your finished blocks A and B, arrange as shown and sew together as you would a Nine-Patch block.

Quilting and Finishing

15. Baste and quilt as desired. The quilt shown used contrasting threads on top and a thread to match the backing in the bobbin.

16. Attach your preferred method of hanging device for mini quilts (this quilt has folded squares in the top corners). Sew your binding strips end to end to form one length and bind!

Pick out the colours with your quilting.

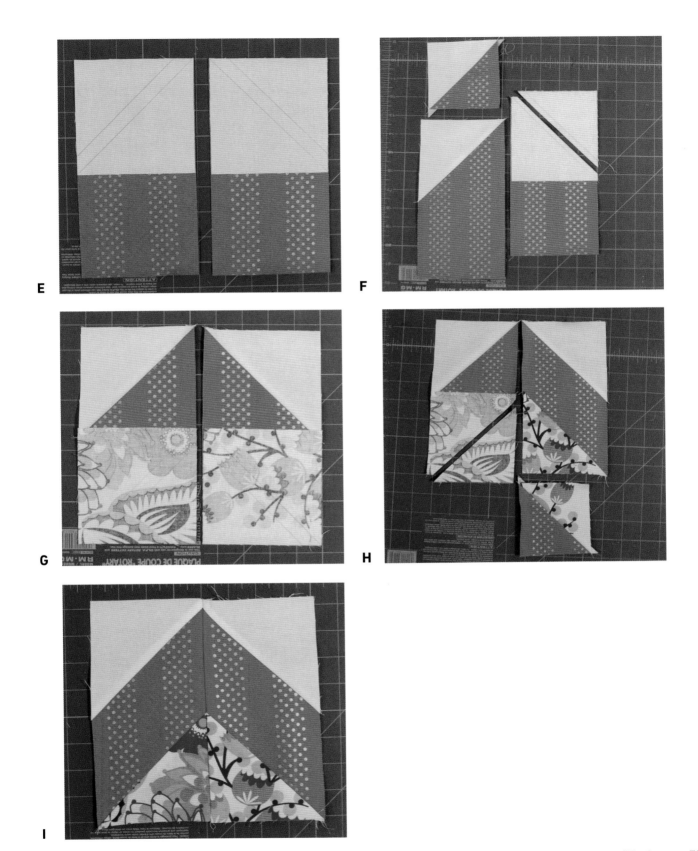

E

F

G

H

I

MINI QUILT

Finished quilt:
13½in square approx

Cutting Out

1. From Fabric A, cut nine (9) 2in squares and seventy-two (72) 1¼in squares.

2. From Fabric B, cut thirty-six (36) 1½in squares and thirty-six (36) 1in squares.

3. From Fabric C, cut seventy-two (72) 1¼in × 2in rectangles.

4. From the background fabric, cut:

• Seventy-two (72) 1¼in squares

• Thirty-six (36) 1½in squares

• Thirty-six (36) 1in squares

• Thirty-six (36) 1in × 2in rectangles

• Thirty-six (36) 1in × 1½in rectangles

5. From the binding fabric, cut two (2) 2¼in × WOF strips.

Piecing the Mini Quilt

6. Repeat Super-Size Block, Steps 6–13 (pages 53 and 54) a total of nine (9) times, then sew your nine mini blocks together as shown in the finished mini quilt. In Step 6, trim HSTs to 1in square.

Quilting and Finishing

7. Baste and quilt as desired, then attach your preferred method of hanging device for mini quilts. Sew your binding strips end to end to form one length and bind!

This tiny crosshatch is the perfect finish.

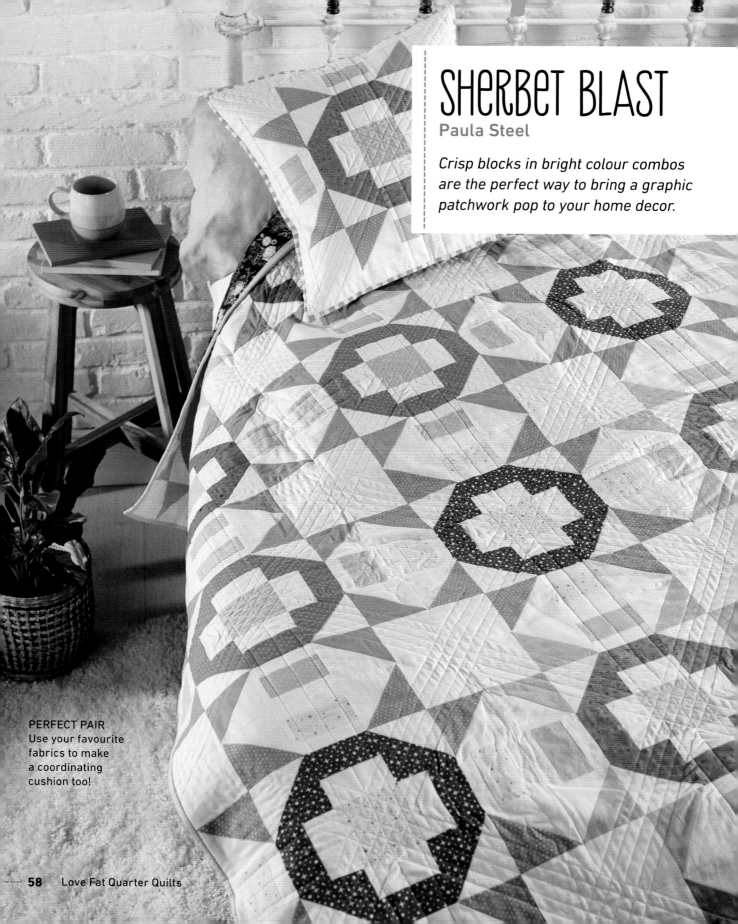

SHERBET BLAST
Paula Steel

Crisp blocks in bright colour combos are the perfect way to bring a graphic patchwork pop to your home decor.

PERFECT PAIR
Use your favourite fabrics to make a coordinating cushion too!

QUILT

Finished quilt: 60in × 75in

TOP TIP
Complement the angular patchwork design with diagonal quilting lines.

You Will Need

Dark mint: One (1) fat quarter

Dark peach:
One (1) fat quarter

Dark yellow:
One (1) fat quarter

Dark blue: One (1) fat quarter

Medium mint:
One (1) fat quarter

Medium peach:
One (1) fat quarter

Medium yellow:
One (1) fat quarter

Medium blue:
One (1) fat quarter

Light mint: One (1) fat quarter

Light peach:
One (1) fat quarter

Light yellow:
One (1) fat quarter

Light blue: One (1) fat quarter

Background fabric: 3½yds

Backing fabric: 3¾yds

Binding fabric: ½yd

Batting: 66in × 81in

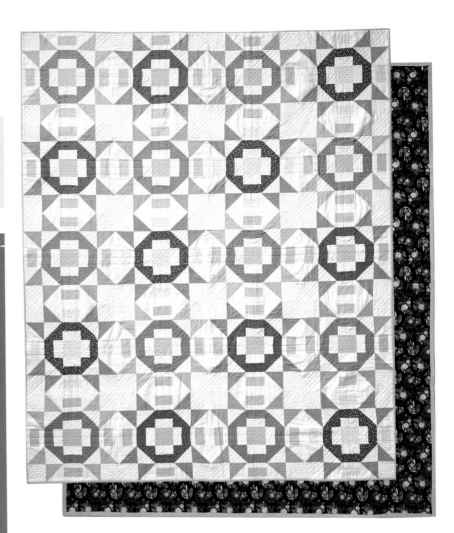

NOTES
- Seam allowance are ¼in throughout, unless otherwise noted.
- Press seams open throughout, unless otherwise stated.
- Press fabrics well before cutting.
- RST = right side together
- WOF = width of fabric
- HST = half-square triangle

Cutting Out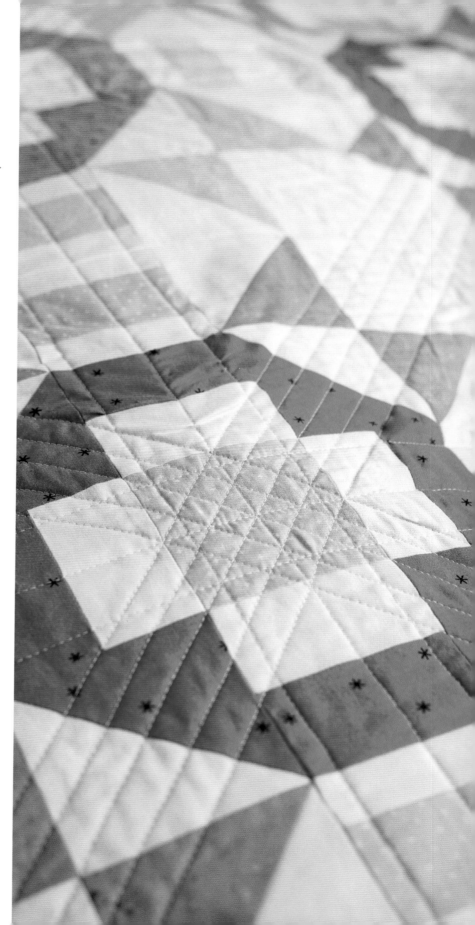

1. From each of the four dark colours, cut:

- Ten (10) 4in squares

- Four (4) 2in × 18in

2. From each of the four medium colours, cut:

- Twenty (20) 4in squares

3. From each of the four light colours, cut:

- Five (5) 3½in squares

- Four (4) 2in × 18in

4. From the background fabric, cut:

- Sixteen (16) 1¼in × WOF

- Eight (8) 2in × WOF

- Eighty (80) 3½in squares

- One hundred and twenty (120) 4in squares

5. From the binding fabric, cut:

- Seven (7) 2½in × WOF

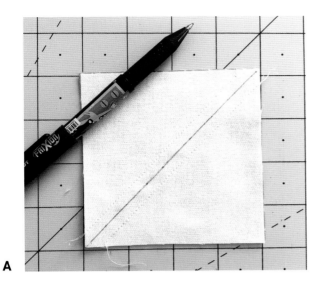

A

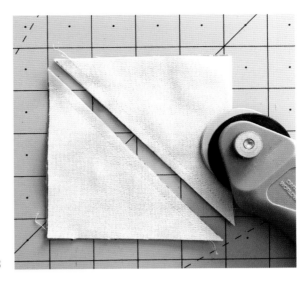

B

Preparing the HST Units

6. Draw a line diagonally on the wrong side of each background 4in square. *Fig. A*

Place each square RST with one of the coloured 4in squares and sew ¼in each side of the drawn line. Cut along the drawn line to make two HSTs from each square. *Fig. B*

7. Press the HSTs open, pressing the seams towards the coloured fabric. Trim each HST to 3½in square, aligning the diagonal seam with the 45-degree line of your quilt ruler. *Fig. C*

8. Once you have sewn all the HSTs, you should have forty medium/background fabric HSTs and twenty dark/background fabric HSTs for each colour.

Preparing the Dark Striped Blocks

9. Take the eight 2in × WOF background strips and cut in half to make sixteen strips, each approx 21in long.

10. Take one of the background 2in strips, and sew to a dark 2in × 18in strip along the long edge. *Note:* The background strip will be longer than the coloured strip. Press the seam open. Subcut five 3½in squares from the strip. *Fig. D*

11. Repeat Step 10 (above) with the remaining dark strips to make a total of twenty dark striped squares for each colour.

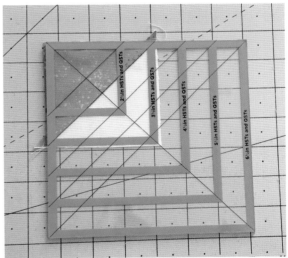

C

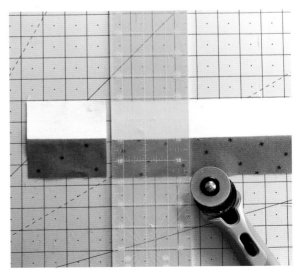

D

Preparing the Light Striped Blocks

12. Take the sixteen 1¼in × WOF background strips and cut in half to make a total of thirty two strips, each approx 21in long.

13. Sew a background strip to either side of a light 2in × 18in strip. Press the seams open, and subcut into five 3½in squares. *Fig. E*

14. Repeat Step 13 with the remaining light strips, to make a total of twenty light striped squares for each colour.

Piecing the Block

15. Take four dark blue HSTs, eight medium blue HSTs, four dark blue striped squares, four light yellow striped squares, four background 3½in squares, and one light yellow 3½in square.

Arrange as shown. *Fig. F*

16. Sew the squares together in rows, then join the rows, carefully matching seam allowances to complete one block.

17. Repeat the process in Steps 15 and 16 (above) to make a total of five blocks in each of the colour combinations:

- Dark and medium blue with light yellow
- Dark and medium peach with light mint
- Dark and medium yellow with light blue
- Dark and medium mint with light peach

Assembling the Quilt Top

18. Arrange the blocks in five rows of four blocks, referring to the photography for colour placement. Sew the blocks into rows, pressing the seams open. Then sew the five rows together to complete the quilt top, pressing seams open or to one side as preferred.

E

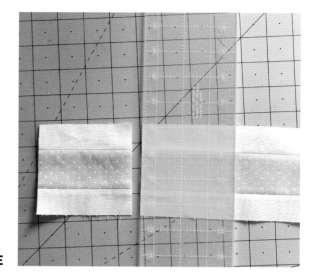

F

Quilting and Finishing

19. Cut the backing fabric in half across the width. Remove the selvedges and sew the two pieces together using a ½in seam. Press the seam open.

20. Press the quilt top and backing well. Make a quilt sandwich by placing the backing fabric right side down, the batting on top, then place the quilt top centrally and right side up. Baste the layers together using your preferred method.

21. Quilt as desired. The quilt shown was quilted in simple straight lines echoing the diagonals and straight lines, using a light coloured thread. Trim off the excess batting and backing fabric, and square up the quilt.

22. Sew the binding strips together end to end using diagonal seams. Press the seams open and trim away the dog-ears. Fold in half lengthways, wrong sides together, and press.

23. Sew the binding to the right side of the quilt, creating a neat mitre at each corner. Fold the binding over to the back of the quilt and hand stitch in place around the edge to finish.

CUSHION

Finished cushion:
18in square

TOP TIP
Add a splash of fun to your coordinating cushion with a cute stripy binding!

You Will Need

Dark peach: One (1) fat eighth

Medium mint:
One (1) fat eighth

Light yellow:
One (1) fat eighth

Light blue: 3½in square

Cushion backing fabric: ½yd

Binding fabric:
One (1) fat quarter

Batting: 20in square

Cutting Out

1. From the dark peach, cut:

• Two (2) 4in squares

• One (1) 2in × 15in

2. From the medium mint fabric, cut:

• Four (4) 4in squares

3. From the light yellow fabric, cut:

• One (1) 2in × 15in

4. From the light blue fabric, cut:

• One (1) 3½in square

5. From the background fabric, cut:

• Two (2) 1¼in × 15in

• One (1) 2in × 15in

• Four (4) 3½in squares

• Six (6) 4in squares

• Two (2) 15½in × 2in

• Two (2) 18½in × 2in

6. From the binding fabric, cut:

• Five (5) 2in × 22in

7. From the cushion backing fabric, cut:

• Two (2) 13in × 18½in

Piecing the Cushion Front

8. Follow Preparing the HST Units, Steps 6 and 7 (page 61) to make four dark peach/background HSTs and eight medium mint/background HSTs.

9. Sew the dark peach and background 2in × 15in strips along the long edges. Press open and subcut into four 3½in squares.

10. Sew the background 1¼in × 15in strips to either side of the light yellow 2in × 15in strip. Press the seams open and subcut into four 3½in squares.

11. Arrange the HSTs and striped squares with the remaining 3½in background and light blue squares in five rows of five, referring to the photography for placement. Sew together in rows, then sew the five rows together, carefully matching seams.

12. Sew the 2in × 15½in background strips to either side of the block. Sew the 2in × 18½in strips to the top and bottom to complete the cushion front.

Quilting and Finishing

13. Place the cushion front on top of your batting and baste in place. Quilt as desired. The cushion shown was marked and quilted in diagonal and vertical lines using a Hera marker. Trim away the excess batting and square up the cushion front.

14. Take one cushion back piece and press under ½in twice along one long edge. Topstitch in place to hem. Repeat with the second cushion back piece.

15. With the cushion front right side down, place the two backing pieces on top, both right side up. Align the raw edges with the edges of the cushion front, with hemmed edges overlapping in the centre. Baste around the outer edge.

16. Join the binding strips into one long length, using diagonal seams. Press the seam open, trim the dog-ears, and press in half lengthwise WST.

17. Attach the binding to the front of the cushion in the same way as you would for a quilt, mitring the corners and joining the two ends. Fold the binding over to the back of the cushion and hand stitch in place to finish. This cushion has a very narrow binding to create a piped look.

PRINT PATTERN
Svetlana Sotak

Stitch up some simple HRTs in pretty prints; then mix them up into a supersize diamond design!

BRILLIANT BINDING
Use a bold graphic binding fabric for a super-colourful finish.

QUILT

Finished quilt:
57in × 76in approx

Fabrics used: Print fabrics are from the Lavish collection by Katarina Roccella for Art Gallery Fabrics; background fabric is White from the Kona Cotton Solids collection by Robert Kaufman.

TOP TIP
Get colourful with mix and match prints or try tonal shades for a 3D effect!

You Will Need

Background fabric (white): 2¾yds

Print fabrics: One (1) fat quarter each of six (6) different prints

Backing fabric: 4¾yds

Batting: 63in × 82in

Binding fabric: ½yd

NOTES
- Seam allowances are ¼in, unless otherwise noted.
- HRT = half-rectangle triangle
- RST = right sides together
- WOF = width of fabric
- WST = wrong sides together

Cutting Out

1. From the background fabric, cut:

- Four (4) 11in × WOF strips. Subcut to give twenty-four (24) 6½in × 11in rectangles.

- Three (3) 7in × WOF strips

- Three (3) 9in × WOF strips

2. From each print fabric fat quarter, cut four (4) 6½in × 11in rectangles to give a total of twenty-four (24) rectangles.

3. From the binding fabric, cut seven (7) 2½in × WOF strips.

Small-scale prints are perfect for the supersize diamonds.

Making the HRT Units

4. Take twelve background 6½in × 11in rectangles and twelve print 6½in × 11in rectangles (two of each print). Cut each one in half diagonally from the top left to the bottom right corner to give a total of twenty-four background rectangles and twenty-four print rectangles. *Fig. A*

5. Take the remaining background and print 6½in × 11in rectangles. Cut each one in half diagonally from the top right to the bottom left corner to give a total of twenty-four background rectangles and twenty-four print rectangles. *Fig. B*

A

B

6. Take one background triangle and one print triangle from Step 4. Place them RST, pin, and then stitch together along the diagonal edge. The triangles will be offset by approx ¼in at the points. *Fig. C*

7. Flip open and press the seam towards the print fabric, then trim the unit to 6in × 10½in. *Fig. D*

8. Repeat Steps 6 and 7 (above) with the remaining triangles from Step 4 to make a total of twenty-four HRT units.

9. Repeat Steps 6–8 (above) with the triangles from Step 5 to make a total of twenty-four HRT units.

C

D

Assembling the Quilt Top

10. Arrange your units into six rows of eight HRTs each, referring to the photograph for placement. Each row has four of each type of HRT, arranged alternately with some of the units rotated by 180 degrees.

11. Join the units into rows using a ¼in seam allowance, then join the rows using a ⅜in seam allowance.

12. Take the three 7in × WOF background strips and join end to end with straight seams. Subcut to give two (2) 7in × 59¼in strips. Join these strips to each side of the quilt centre.

13. Take the three 9in × WOF background strips and join end to end with straight seams. Subcut to give two (2) 57½in × 9in strips. Join these strips to the top and bottom of the quilt centre to complete the quilt top.

Quilting and Finishing

14. Cut the backing fabric in half across the width. Remove the selvedges and re-join the pieces along the length with a ½in seam. Press the seam open.

15. Press the quilt top and backing well. Make a quilt sandwich by placing the backing fabric right side down, the batting on top, then the quilt top centrally and right side up. The backing and batting are slightly larger than the quilt top. Baste the layers together using your preferred method.

16. Quilt as desired. The quilt shown was quilted in vertical lines.

17. Trim off the excess batting and backing fabric, and square up the quilt.

18. Sew the binding strips together using diagonal seams. Press the seams open and trim away the dog-ears. Fold in half lengthwise, WST, and press.

19. Sew the binding to the right side of the quilt, folding a mitre at each corner.

20. Fold the binding over to the back of the quilt and hand stitch in place to finish.

BLUEBERRY PARK

Karen Lewis

Karen mixes up the fresh peach, sky blue, and lime green tones of her collection on a light grey background quilt.

BACK TO FRONT
This stylish quilt reverses the background and feature fabrics to stunning effect.

QUILT

Finished quilt:
54in × 72in approx

Fabrics used: Blueberry Park collection designed by Karen Lewis for Robert Kaufman

You Will Need

Print fabric:
Twelve (12) fat quarters

Background fabric: 2½yds

Backing fabric: 60in × 80in

Batting: 60in × 80in

Binding fabric: ½yd

NOTES

- Seam allowances are ¼in, unless otherwise noted.
- HST = half-square triangle
- Press all fabrics well before cutting.
- Press seams open, unless otherwise instructed.

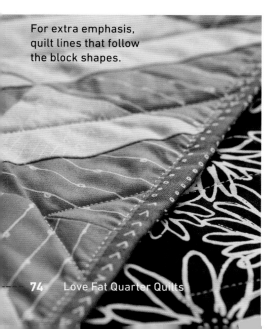

For extra emphasis, quilt lines that follow the block shapes.

Karen's stunning collection for Robert Kaufman offers an extensive palette of greys alongside on-trend colours, from coral to cadet to canary.

Cutting Out

1. From each of the twelve print fabrics, cut four (4) 3½in squares and twelve (12) 4in squares.

2. From the background fabric, cut ninety-six (96) 3½in squares and one hundred and fourty-four (144) 4in squares.

3. From the binding fabric, cut seven (7) 2½in × WOF strips.

Piecing the Blocks

4. Match a 4in square of print fabric RST with a 4in square of background fabric. Make two HST units by marking a diagonal line on the back and sewing with a ¼in seam on either side of the line. Cut along the line and press open, then trim to 3½in square. Repeat with all remaining 4in squares.

5. Take six (6) matching HSTs and one 3½in square of the same print and arrange with two background squares, as shown.

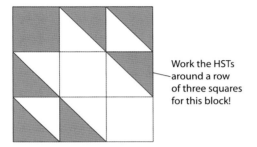

Work the HSTs around a row of three squares for this block!

Join the squares in rows, then sew the rows together. Repeat to create a total of forty-eight (48) blocks.

Assembling the Quilt

6. Lay out your blocks in eight (8) rows of six (6) blocks, rotating them as shown in the photo to create the pattern. Sew each of the rows together. Press the seams open and sew the rows together, again pressing the seams when you are done.

Quilting and Finishing

7. Make up a quilt sandwich with the quilt top, backing, and batting, then baste using your preferred method. Quilt as desired—the quilt shown was quilted in a series of diagonal lines to emphasise the block shapes.

8. Trim away any excess batting and backing fabric, and square up the quilt ready for binding. Join the binding strips together into one long length and use this as a double-fold binding for your quilt to finish.

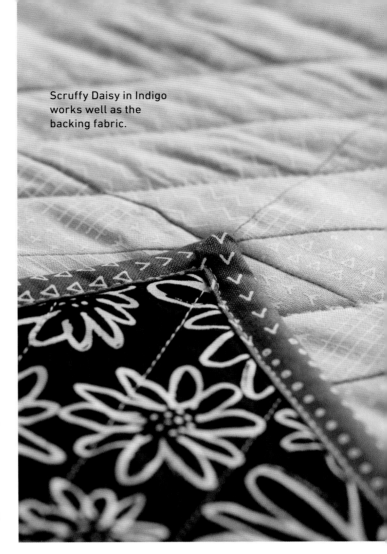

Scruffy Daisy in Indigo works well as the backing fabric.

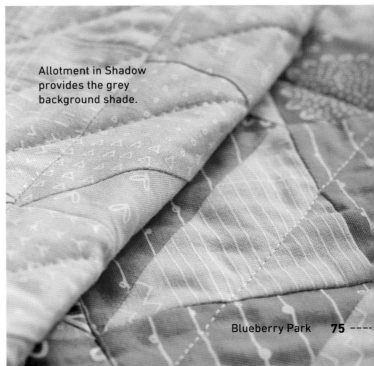

Allotment in Shadow provides the grey background shade.

TOP TIP
Use up your scraps
by making super-
cute coasters!

CUSHION

Finished cushion:
18in square

You Will Need

Print fabrics: Four (4) fabrics, 8in square

Background fabric: ¼yd

Backing fabric: Two (2) 18½in × 12in

Batting: 20in square

Cushion pad: 18in

Cutting Out

1. From each of the print fabrics, cut one (1) 3½ square and three (3) 4in squares.

2. From the background fabric, cut eight (8) 3½ squares and twelve (12) 4in squares for the HSTs.

Choose one fabric to match the room and the rest is up to you!

Assembling the Cushion

3. Make four (4) blocks as in Piecing the Blocks, Steps 4 and 5 (page 75).

4. Lay out the four blocks as shown in the photo and sew together. Press all the seams open.

5. Baste onto the batting and quilt as desired—the cushion shown was quilted in diagonal straight lines in each quarter.

The cushion's quilt lines follow the 'X' shape for definition.

Assembling the Cushions

6. Sew a ½in double-fold hem along the long edge of each backing piece.

7. Arrange the two backing pieces, right sides together with the pillow front, overlapping the hems in the centre. Pin, then stitch around the edges. Turn right sides out and press.

TONAL TREES
Lindsey Neill

Pick out colour block solids to make a minimalist quilt using some simple FPP and clever appliqué.

HIGH IMPACT
Simple shapes and negative space make this stand-out design.

QUILT

Finished quilt:
49½in × 55¼in approx

You Will Need

Background fabric (white):
3yds

Fabric A (turquoise):
Three (3) 7in squares

Fabric B (aqua):
One (1) 7in square

Fabric C (green):
One (1) fat quarter

Fabric D (lime):
One (1) fat quarter

Fabric E (orange):
Three (3) 7in squares

Fabric F (yellow):
One (1) 7in square

Fabric G (pink):
Three (3) 7in squares

Fabric H (red):
One (1) 7in square

¼in wide single-fold bias tape (black): 3yds

Backing fabric: 3¼yds

Batting: 56in × 60in

Binding fabric: ½yd

Templates: One (1) copy of each FPP Templates A–D

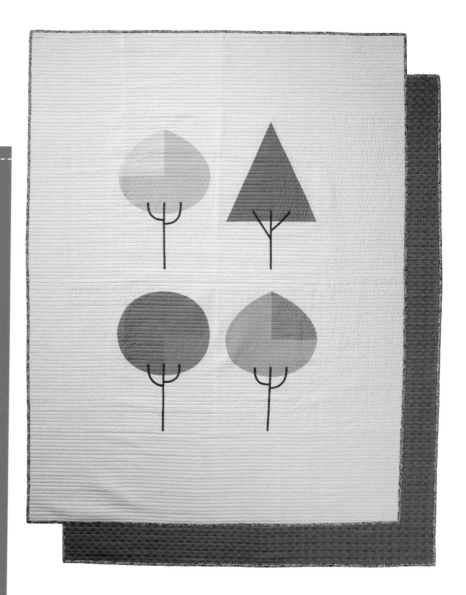

NOTES

- Seam allowances are ¼in, unless otherwise noted.
- Templates include seam allowances, where necessary.
- FPP = foundation paper piecing
- RST = right sides together
- WOF = width of fabric
- WST = wrong sides together
- Where a cutting instruction indicates to cut the reverse, flip the template over on the fabric before cutting.
- Where there are markings on the template, transfer them over to the right side of your fabric to identify the orientation of each shape. Lindsey recommends using a water-soluble pen for this.
- For templates, see Downloadable Patterns (page 93).
- Quilted by Sarah Wilson of Crinklelove

Cutting Out

1. From the white fabric, cut:

- Two (2) Circle Tree Arches, using the template

- Two (2) Circle Tree Arches reverse, using the template

- Two (2) Teardrop Tree Top Arches, using the template

- Two (2) Teardrop Tree Top Arches reverse, using the template

- Two (2) Teardrop Tree Bottom Arches, using the template

- Two (2) Teardrop Tree Bottom Arches reverse, using the template

- Two (2) 8in × WOF strips. Subcut to give three (3) 14½in × 8in rectangles and one (1) 14½in × 5½in rectangle.

- One (1) 28½in × 2¾in strip

- Two (2) 11¼in × WOF strips. Trim to give two (2) 11¼in × 42¾in strips.

- Three (3) 12in × WOF strips. Subcut one (1) strip in half widthwise and sew one half to one (1) 12in × WOF strip and the other half to the remaining 12in × WOF strip. Trim to give two (2) 50in × 12in strips.

- Two (2) 8in × 8¾in rectangles for section 2 on FPP Templates A and B

- Two (2) 5¼in × 8¾in rectangles for section 2 on FPP Templates C and D

2. From Fabric A, using the templates, cut:

- One (1) Teardrop Tree Top

- One (1) Teardrop Tree Bottom

- One (1) Teardrop Tree Bottom reverse

3. From Fabric B, using the template, cut one (1) Teardrop Tree Top reverse.

4. From Fabric C, cut:

- One (1) 4½in × 10⅜in rectangle. Cut in half diagonally from corner to corner to give two (2) triangles—you will only need one for section 1 on the FPP Template A.

- One 7in × 8¾in rectangle for section 1 on the FPP Template C

5. From Fabric D, cut:

- One (1) 4½in × 10⅜in rectangle. Cut in half diagonally from corner to corner to give two (2) triangles—you will only need one for section 1 on the FPP Template B.

- One 7in × 8¾in rectangle for section 1 on FPP Template D

6. From Fabric E, using the templates, cut one (1) Circle Tree Quarter and two (2) Circle Tree Quarters reverse.

7. From Fabric F, using the template, cut one (1) Circle Tree Quarter.

8. From Fabric G, using the templates, cut:

- One (1) Teardrop Tree Top reverse

- One (1) Teardrop Tree Bottom

- One (1) Teardrop Tree Bottom reverse

9. From Fabric H, using the template, cut one (1) Teardrop Tree Top.

10. From the binding fabric, cut six (6) 2½in × WOF strips.

TOP TIP

Lindsey's trees use two shades of each colour— you could use more for a super-tonal effect.

Piecing the Circle Tree

11. Take one Circle Tree Quarter fabric piece and, WST, fold it in half, finger pressing to create a midpoint crease on the curved edge. Take one corresponding Circle Tree Arch fabric piece and, RST, fold it in half, finger-pressing to create a midpoint crease on the curved edge. *Fig. A*

12. Place the two pieces RST with the Arch piece on top. The orientation marks should be next to each other and the midpoint creases should nest. Pin in place at the midpoints. *Fig. B*

13. Match up the side edges of the pieces and then pin the ends of the curved seam in place. Smooth out the excess fabric and pin in place. *Fig. C*

14. With the Arch piece on top, carefully sew along the curved edge. *Fig. D*

Press the seam towards the clam piece to make one Circle Tree unit, which should measure 7½in × 7in. *Fig. E*

15. Repeat Steps 11–14 (above) with the remaining Circle Tree Quarters and Quarters reverse to make a total of four Circle Tree units.

16. Join the four Circle Tree units in a two-by-two layout. Press the seams open. Trim ½in from the bottom edge of the Circle Tree block, making sure not to trim the edge of the tree. *Fig. F*

17. Join a 14½in × 8in background rectangle to the bottom edge of the trimmed Circle Tree block. Press the seam towards the background rectangle to complete the Circle Tree block, which should now measure 14½in × 20½in. *Fig. G*

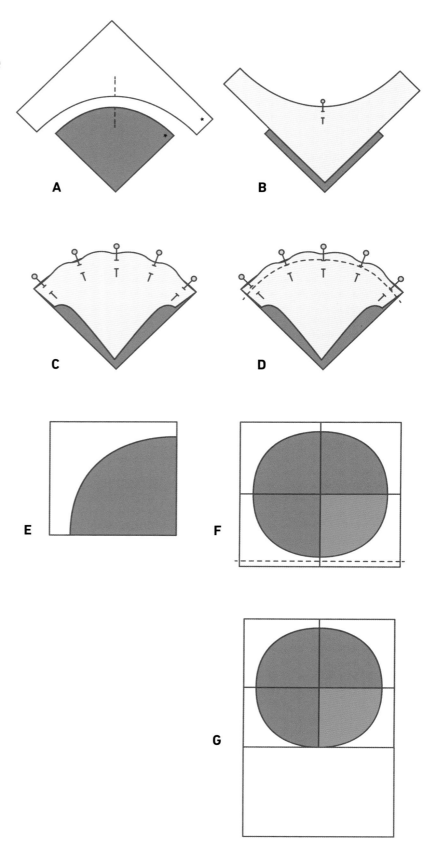

A

B

C

D

E

F

G

Piecing the Teardrop Trees

18. Repeat Steps 11–14 (previous page) with the Teardrop Tree Top, Top reverse, Bottom, and Bottom reverse Fabric A and Fabric B pieces to make a total of four Teardrop Tree units. The Tree Top pieces will need to extend ¼in past the arch piece. Each top unit should measure 7½in × 7¾in. Each bottom unit should measure 7½in × 6½in. *Fig. H*

19. Join the four Teardrop Tree units in a two-by-two layout. Press the seams open. Trim ¼in from the bottom edge of the Teardrop Tree block, making sure not to trim the edge of the tree.

20. Join a 14½in × 8in background rectangle to the bottom edge of the trimmed block. Press the seam towards the background rectangle to complete one Teardrop Tree block, which should now measure 14½in × 20½in. *Figs. I-J*

21. Repeat Steps 18–20 (above) with the Fabric G and Fabric H Teardrop Tree pieces to make a second Teardrop Tree.

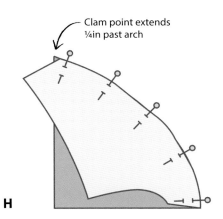

Clam point extends ¼in past arch

H

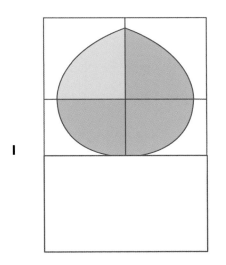

I

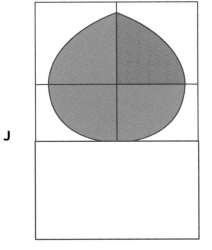

J

Piecing the Triangle Tree

22. Take the FPP Template A, the Fabric C triangle for section 1, and the background rectangle for section 2. Position the section 1 fabric piece right side up and centred over section 1 on the unprinted side of the FPP template, then pin in place.

23. Now place the section 2 fabric piece RST on the section 1 fabric piece, matching up the raw edges where sections 1 and 2 will be joined. Check that, when flipped over at the seamline, the new fabric will cover section 2 plus at least ¼in all around. Pin in place.

24. Turn the template over and stitch on the marked line between sections 1 and 2, extending the line by a few stitches at each end of the seamline. Fold back the paper and trim the seam allowance to ¼in. Flip the section 2 fabric piece open and press well. Trim on the outer line of the template and then carefully remove the template.

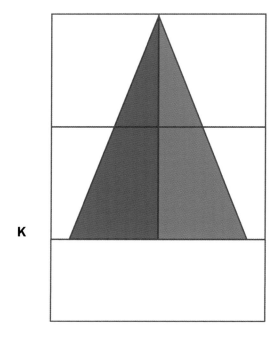

K

25. Repeat Steps 22–24 (above) for the FPP Templates B, C, and D. Each unit should measure 7½in × 8in.

26. Join the A–D units into a two-by-two layout. Press the seams open.

27. Join a 14½in × 5½in background rectangle to the bottom edge of the block. Press the seam towards the background rectangle to complete one Triangle Tree block, which should now measure 14½in × 20½in. *Fig. K*

Appliquéing the Tree Trunks

28. Take the bias tape and measure the length you need for the trunk of one tree. The top of the trunk should extend into the tree and the bottom of the trunk should be level with the bottom raw edge of the block. Add ¼in and then cut. Fold under one short raw edge by ¼in and press. Repeat to make trunks for the remaining three trees.

29. Repeat Step 28 (above) to make two branches for each tree, this time adding ½in after measuring. The branches need to be different lengths so that they don't overlap on the trunk, and can be different shapes.

30. Baste the branches to the quilt, making sure that the neatened end is against the tree—Lindsey recommends using washable glue for this. Baste the bias tape for the trunks on top, making sure that the neatened end is against the tree and that the raw edges of the branches are hidden underneath the trunk. Appliqué the trunk and branches in place by sewing along the perimeter of the bias tape.

Get creative with appliqué to make different tree trunks.

Assembling the Quilt Top

31. Join the tree blocks together into pairs. Press the seams open. Join the pairs of blocks with the 28½in × 2¾in background strip between them. Press the seams towards the background fabric.

32. Join a 11¼in × 42¾in background strip to each side of the quilt centre, and then join a 50in × 12in background strip to the top and bottom.

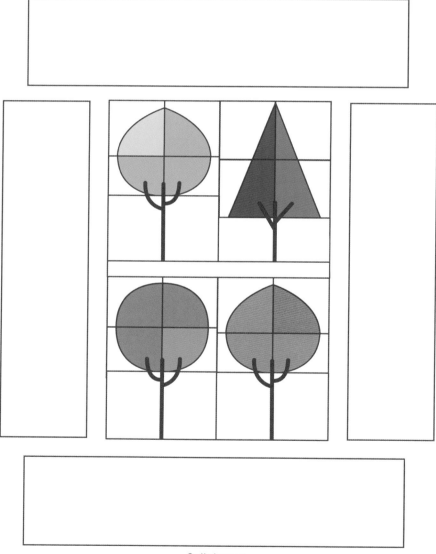

Quilt layout

Quilting and Finishing

33. Cut the backing fabric in half across the width. Remove the selvedges and re-join the pieces along the length with a ½in seam. Press the seam open.

34. Press the quilt top and backing well. Make a quilt sandwich by placing the backing fabric right side down, the batting on top, then the quilt top centrally and right side up. The backing and batting are slightly larger than the quilt top. Baste the layers together using your preferred method.

35. Quilt as desired—this quilt was quilted with horizontal straight lines by Sarah Wilson of Crinklelove.

36. Trim off the excess batting and backing, and square up the quilt.

37. Sew the binding strips together end to end using diagonal seams. Press the seams open and trim away the dog-ears. Fold in half lengthwise, WST, and press.

38. Sew the binding to the right side of the quilt, folding a mitre at each corner.

39. Fold the binding over to the back of the quilt and hand stitch in place to finish.

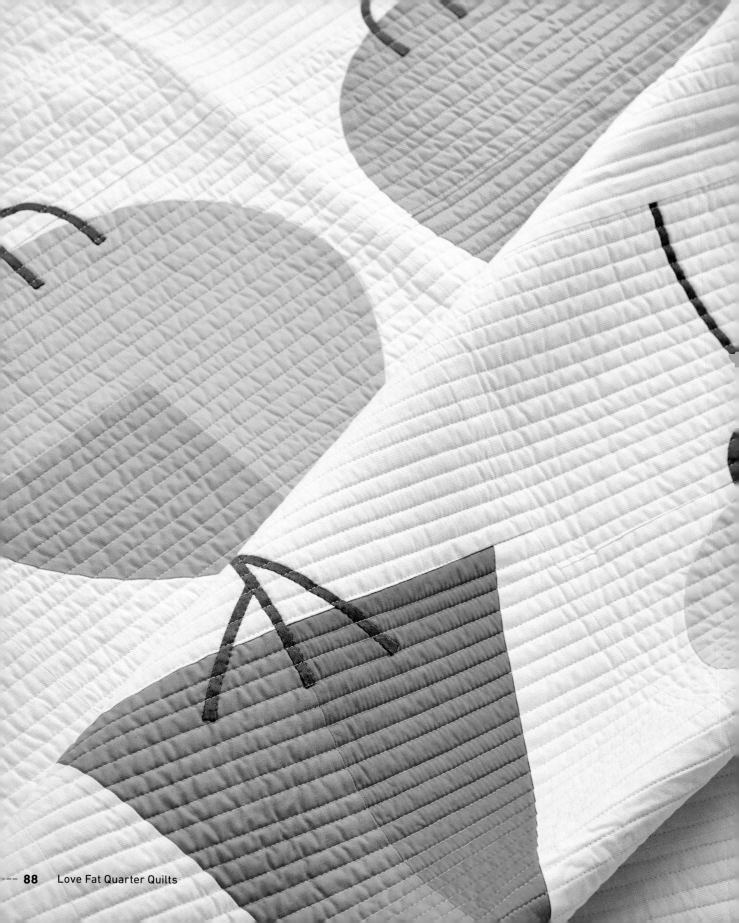

RAINBOW ROWS

Karen Lewis

Keep it simple and let the colour do the talking with this quick-stitch quilt top.

Easy-peasy piecing!

PRINTS PLEASE
We can't get enough of Karen's screen printed fabrics—the white ink really pops on those bright Kona cottons. Add alternating white squares, and you've got a match made in heaven!

QUILT

Finished quilt:
48in × 64in approx

Fabric used: Coloured fabrics are Kona Cottons hand printed by Karen; backing fabric is Sun Print × and Plus by Alison Glass.

NOTES

- Seam allowances are ¼in throughout, unless otherwise noted.
- Wash and press all of your fabrics well before cutting.
- Press seams open, unless otherwise instructed.
- WOF = width of fabric
- FQ = fat quarter

This simple layout is all about the colour—so throw caution to the wind and be brave!

Cutting Out

1. From the white fabric, cut three hundred and eighty four (384) 2½in squares. The simplest way to do this is to cut into 2½in strips and then stack a few strips and subcut into 2½in squares.

2. From each fat quarter, cut fifty-five (55) 2½in squares. You will actually only need 54 from the last FQ.

3. From your binding fabric, cut six (6) 2½in × WOF binding strips.

Assembling the Quilt

4. Arrange the squares into thirty-two (32) rows, each containing twenty-four (24) fabric squares. Alternate one coloured square with one white square, following the layout diagram (below).

5. Sew each of the rows together. Press the seams open and then sew the rows together, again pressing the seams when you are done.

TOP TIP

This checker board design works great with print fabrics—dive into your stash for a scrappy finish!

Speed Piecing

This project is perfect for chain piecing. Stitch the first two squares from each row, without snipping the threads between. Repeat with pairs of squares working across the rows, then start joining the pairs until all your squares have been sewn. There is no need to snip the threads between the squares until all of the rows are complete—this will also keep your squares from getting mixed up as you sew!

Join the first pair from each row …

… sew the next pair and add to the first.

Quilt layout

Quilting and Finishing

6. Make a quilt sandwich of the backing fabric, right side down; the batting; and the quilt top, right side up. Smooth the layers and then pin or spray baste them together. Quilt as desired. The quilt shown was quilted in a grid design to accentuate the patchwork layout of the quilt.

7. Trim off the excess batting and backing fabric, and square up the quilt ready for binding. Join the binding strips together into one long length, and use this as a double-fold binding for your quilt. Bind, taking care to mitre the corners.

Play with tones within each colour group.

This Alison Glass print is lovely for the quilt back.

ABOUT THE CONTRIBUTORS

Check out these contributor websites for more great content! For additional resources, visit *Love Patchwork & Quilting* at lovepatchworkandquilting.com.

Jo Avery
(United Kingdom)

Print Spin (page 12) originally appeared in issue 59 of *Love Patchwork & Quilting*.

Website: joavery.co.uk

Instagram: @joaverystitch

Nicole Calver
(Canada)

Clippings (page 51) originally appeared in issue 28 of *Love Patchwork & Quilting*.

Website: snipssnippets.ca

Instagram: @snipssnippets

Karen Lewis
(United Kindgom)

Pixel Diamonds (page 6), *Hourglass Twist* (page 45), *Blueberry Park* (page 73), and *Rainbow Rows* (page 89) originally appeared in issues 5, 10, 28, and 17 of *Love Patchwork & Quilting*.

Website: karenlewistextiles.com

Instagram: @karenlewistextiles

Facebook: /karenlewistextiles

Lindsey Neill
(United States)

Tonal Trees (page 79) originally appeared in issue 46 of *Love Patchwork & Quilting*.

Website: penandpaperpatterns.com

Instagram: @penandpaperpatterns

Facebook: /penandpaperpatterns

Laura Pritchard
(United Kingdom)

Earn Your Stripes (page 30) originally appeared in issue 28 of *Love Patchwork & Quilting*.

Instagram: @laurapritchardquilts

Felice Regina
(United States)

Pixel Pop (page 36) originally appeared in issue 65 of *Love Patchwork & Quilting*.

Svetlana Sotak
(Netherlands)

Print Pattern (page 67) originally appeared in issue 42 of *Love Patchwork & Quilting*.

Website: sotakhandmade.blogspot.com

Instagram: @sotakhandmade

Susan Standen
(United Kingdom)

Let's Get Cosy (page 18) originally appeared in issue 14 of *Love Patchwork & Quilting*.

Website: canadianabroad-susan.blogspot.com

Instagram: @canadianabroad

Paula Steel
(United Kingdom)

Sherbet Blast (page 58) originally appeared in issue 93 of *Love Patchwork & Quilting*.

Website: paulasteelquilts.com

Instagram: @paulasteel.quilts